THE SECRET ORIGINS

GRANDMASTER CHO

AN ANALYSIS OF CHOI YONG SOOL'S
CLAIM TO DAITO-RYU AIKI-JUJUTSU
ORIGINS AND ITS EFFECTS ON THE
EARLY DEVELOPMENT OF HAPKIDO

By

Grant A. Miller

January 13, 2016

STATEMENT BY THE AUTHOR

SECRET ORIGINS OF HAPKIDO

GRANDMASTER

CHOI YONG SOOL

AN ANALYSIS OF CHOI YONG-SOOL'S CLAIM TO DAITO-RYU AIKI-JUJUTSU ORIGINS AND ITS EFFECTS ON THE EARLY DEVELOPMENT OF HAPKIDO

ABSTRACT

This book will be analyzing Hapkido master Choi Yong-Sool's claim to have studied directly under Daito-Ryu Aiki JuJutsu master Sokaku Takeda, and why this claim to have studied directly from the Takeda family's Daito-Ryu Aiki JuJutsu system is important to establishing not only his legitimacy in teaching the martial art, but also to trace the common roots that Daito-Ryu Aiki JuJutsu, Hapkido and Aikido share by tracing his lineage back to the root tradition.

This book will look at master Choi Yong-Sool's early history, as compiled from his own biography as well as external sources, it will compare and contrast three critical and fundamental techniques used in Hapkido and Aiki-JuJutsu and trace them back to Daito-Ryu Aiki-Jutsu. It will also look at master Ji Han Jae's involvement in the early art and his significant steps taken to make Hapkido a worldwide martial art.

Master Choi Yong-Sool's biography, interview and assertions of having studied Daito-Ryu Aiki JuJutsu has caused great controversy in Daito-Ryu and other Aiki JuJutsu circles. Hapkido practitioners, looking to find the origins of their art, are also confronted with these controversies. This book will look at all sides and combined with the author's own experiences; will present the strongest case of how all these systems are related.

This book will help the trace the valid history and help mend bridges so that organizations and instructors of Hapkido will understand their roots and in addition will help increase relationships between the various related practices that have stemmed from the parent art (Daito-Ryu Aiki JuJutsu), such as Aiki-JuJutsu and Aikido.

In order to maintain consistency, this book will use the term "Master" to represent all titles and ranks for all persons, living or deceased, which are represented in this book. As there are various titles and ranks given to these founders (such as Korean and Japanese terms such as Do Ju Nim, Hanshi, Grandmaster, etc.) and with the various organizations including, excluding, utilizing, not recognizing, etc. etc. these titles, this book will standardize on the use of "master" for the purposes of this book.

Finally I would like to thank Grandmaster John Barton of the King Cobra Aiki-JuJutsu school in Erie, Grandmaster Ken McKenzie, Master Bill LaVoice and everyone involved with the Sin Moo Hapkido organization, without whose help and support this book would never have come to fruition.

INTRODUCTION

I am a practitioner of the Japanese art of Shotokan. In my over 40+ years of martial arts training, I have been exposed to other disciplines, including Aiki-JuJutsu, Aikido, Kendo, Judo, Kung Fu and Tang Soo Do.

I was first exposed to the art of Hapkido during a seminar I attended at an associated Sin Moo Hapkido school with an instructor who had personally trained under master Ji Han Jae. Immediately I recognized the similarities between Hapkido and the two Japanese arts that I had studied previously, Aiki-JuJutsu and Aikido, and needed to learn how this could be. Thus began a journey of discovery of the art of Hapkido and how it ties in with its cousins, the arts of Aiki-JuJutsu and Aikido.

As I began looking into Hapkido, one of the things I quickly realized was that the Japanese organizations of Daito Ryu Aiki JuJutsu and Aikido distanced themselves from their relationship, or supposed relationship, with the style of Hapkido. It made me search further. I was puzzled at how the same Chinese characters, "Aiki" in Japanese and "HapKi" in Korean, were both used in the names ("AiKi" JuJutsu, "HapKi" Do, "AiKi" Do). Surely there must be some connection I thought.

The deeper I dug though, the more controversy I uncovered. I decided to write this research book because I believe that I am uniquely qualified due to my education and past experiences to be objective, I have had training in Aiki-JuJutsu, and being fluent in Japanese.

I do need to give you some back ground information on myself, as it will help immensely with the understanding of the relationship I have with the Japanese and Chinese languages, both spoken and written. A foster family I lived with was Chinese, they would later unofficially adopt me because it was quickly discovered, when I was 10 years old, that I had something of a gift for learning languages quickly. So I became conversant in Cantonese at a very young age. I tried learning Chinese characters on my own, which was pain staking and difficult.

I went to Penn State University and minored in Japanese. I did so because the Chinese that was taught at Penn State was Mandarin, and not the Cantonese that I had learned, and the Mandarin teacher made it known to me that I was not welcome in the class when she heard me speak Cantonese. I was still wanting to learn Chinese characters, and so I began taking Japanese classes.

In my junior year I studied abroad in Japan at Kansai Gaidai University for one year, where I obtained a certificate of proficiency in the language. After graduation, and for the next twelve years, I worked for Tokyu Corporation, a Japanese company.

So with this information you now understand that I have a good understanding not only of the Japanese language but also of the history and culture due to my college studies and work experience.

University

My very first experience with Hapkido goes back to my young days while living in Los Angeles. There was a Hapkido school near to where I lived. I remember seeing the dojang during my bus trips to and from school and seeing the big capitalized letters HAPKIDO, but not really knowing what it was other than it was a Korean art and I saw a bit of it demonstrated in Bruce Lee's movie "Game of Death" with master Ji Han Jae. Outside of this I really had no other idea of what the art was about.

Thus it was when I went to my first Hapkido seminar. I instantly recognized the wrist locks and techniques being used to be very similar to the Aiki-Jitsu I have studied as well as the Aikido I studied in college. I knew that there was a connection, and had to find out what it was.

As you read through this book I am hopeful that you will see that my end result is to validate master Choi's studies, recreate the relationship that these styles have in common, and deliver to the reader a sense of a fraternal brotherhood that should exist between these styles and that can be further developed instead of being driven apart by nationalism or other reasons.

I also hope to show the courage that master Choi and his students displayed in the development of Hapkido in the overbearing shadow of Japanese racism that was pointed at the Korean people during those years of the Japanese occupation of Korea.

I am thankful for Dr. Thomas for offering a place where a book like this could be accepted and published.

Patience

Master Choi, Yong-Sool

EARLY JAPAN INVOLVEMENT

Choi Yong-Sool was born in today's Yong Dong Village in Chungcheongbuk-do, South Korea on November 9th, 1904.

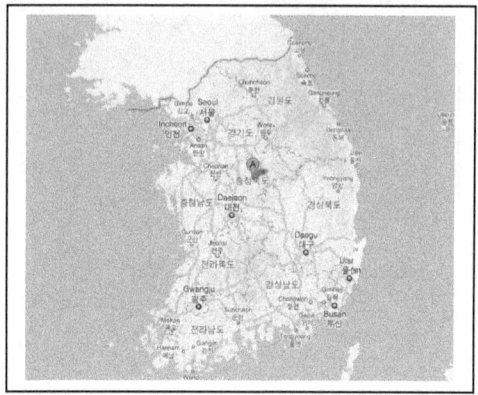

There are conflicting dates as to his actual birthday, however the 11/9/1904 date is the one generally accepted.

He was born into a time just prior to world war I, when the Japanese Meiji Restoration was in full swing westernizing its armed forces and Navy. Korea was occupied by Japan during this time (from 1910). Choi Yong-Sool was taken to Japan at a young age, with no concrete evidence or documentation given as to why.

There is no questioning that he was taken to Japan, but there are questions as to why. According to his biography, he was adopted by the Morimoto family, who were merchants and traders (of sweets) apparently working in Korea in the second year of the Japanese occupation in 1912. This would make Choi Yong-Sool 8 years old, which is in accordance with his biography. According to his biography, Choi resisted the move and while in Japan proved so troublesome that the Morimoto family left him in the streets abandoned. He would later be taken in by an orphanage.

I would like to take a closer look at this adoption. The first matter that I need to clear up in the modern reader's mind is that this is not an adoption as we in the 21st century have come to reason with, for example, where an American family flies to some remote village in China/Vietnam/Russia and adopts an orphaned baby.

Adoption, in context with the period, would simply mean that he lived with the family, he might have called the parents "mother" and "father", but there is no legal document, no court issued adoption books, no CYS to monitor the child, etc. I myself was unofficially adopted by my Chinese foster family. I called the parents "mother" and "father", and my siblings "sisters" and "brothers". To this day I still refer to them as such. But I was never legally adopted by them.

Friend

Choi Yong-Sool's mother and father, if they were still alive in 1912 (and some sources claim that they were deceased), may have saw a better life offered by the Morimoto family in Japan and allowed for the adoption.

However, I would not see it in the terms as "adoption" as we have come to know it, but rather as an adoption for Choi Yong-Sool to learn the trade and craft of the Morimoto family, so he become a productive member of the family in Japan, would have free room and board and in exchange Choi Yong-Sool would work for the family and their business.

The Morimoto family would have a native Korean speaking apprentice learning the trade that they would be able to use in the future in Korea.

If the situation is true, my best speculation about why the Morimoto family offered him employment, apprenticeship and a place to live is most likely they needed a Korean native, a native speaking person that they could train and groom, to head up their Korean operations. While this is speculative, it does give a reason as why Choi Yong-Sool ended up in the streets homeless after being taken to Japan when he resisted the move. The Morimoto family would see Choi Yong-Sool's actions as being that he did not care to follow the path they were providing and therefore, having no further use for him and feeling no obligation since he broke the unwritten contract, left him in the streets.

I would also like to point out that in other sources of his biography, he used the word "abducted" in reference to his being taken from Korea to Japan, which again would lead to his being abandoned if he was not adjusting properly to his new Japanese situation. Abducted or adopted, in either case, he was taken to Japan and found himself homeless.

While the situation of being abandoned is not ideal, it did set Choi Yong-Sool on the path of learning the martial art he would eventually bring home to Korea.

Choi Yong-Sool, out in the streets, resorted to begging. Remember he was probably still just 8 years old or maybe even 9. Eventually he was picked up by the police and taken to a temple (Buddhist) that was acting also as an orphanage. The monk who ran the temple was named Kintaro Watanabe. Life in a temple is not easy, with little of the comforts that life in a home provide. While he was fed and had warm clothing, he would most certainly be working at the temple doing a variety of tasks that were most likely assigned to him and the other orphans that were there.

From my own experiences at temples in Japan, I can say that they are typically cold (with no real heating in the winter) and austere as the monks are trying to live as austere a life as possible. While far better than sleeping on the streets exposed to the elements, it is still a hardship to be in an orphanage. That combined with not being a Japanese native creates an even more difficult daily existence. Choi Yong-Sool was Korean, and even though the monks are caring for him and giving him shelter, there was a very hostile and negative feeling amongst Japanese towards the Koreans.

I may even add my own experience to help enlighten this matter. While at a temple near Kyoto, the monks and visitors were in a line to take a drink from some water from a special well (that was to have some form of cleansing/positive effects). When it came to my turn for a drink, I was denied because my blood was "unclean". I know that it does not really make any sense to deny me, and this was in 1986, but this should give you some idea and if we extrapolate it back to 1912 just imagine what it was like for Choi Yong-Sool while Japan was in its hey-day of the Meiji restoration and military victories.

According to Choi Yong-Sool's biography the two years he spent at the temple were trouble filled and hard. Not having been schooled in Japanese language, he would have found it very difficult to learn how to read and write in Japanese, as well as speak with any degree of sophisticated command of the language.

The difficulty in learning Japanese (written) is that the Japanese use two different alphabets, the first is Hiragana, which descended from the woman's written language and became the alphabet of choice for writing words which are Japanese in origin. The second alphabet is the Katakana alphabet, descended from the male's written language and came to be used as the alphabet for writing foreign words.

In addition, the Japanese utilized Chinese characters as well (rough average estimate for a high school student would be that he/she would need to know 2,000-3,000 Chinese characters to be relatively fluent in the written language).

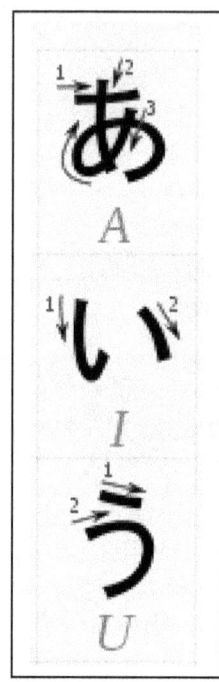 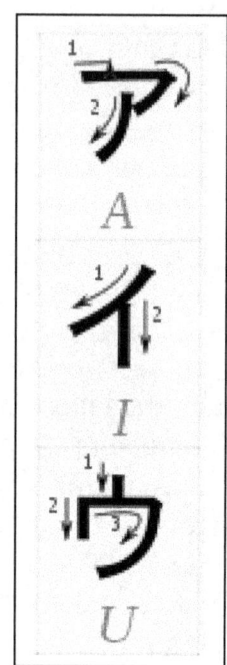

*Three letters (A, I, U) written in
the Hiragana (left) and Katagana alphabets.*

The Korean language, while also using Chinese characters, has its own alphabet (Hangul) which is completely different to the two Japanese alphabets (Hiragana and Katagana). At 8 years old, it is questionable how much schooling Choi had in Korea. There are some sources that state he was illiterate. It is highly probable that Choi Yong-Sool was unable to read/write basic Japanese initially, and he would need to learn the alphabets prior to his being able to read and write. Some sources claim that he was educated during the two years he was living at the temple (did he learn at the temple or did he go to school?).

I am not sure and somewhat skeptical if the monks taught him how to write Japanese, and question if they would invest the amount of time needed for him to learn how to read and write the language. If he went to a public school, he would have been at a significant disadvantage with the other children in terms of reading and writing. My thought is they most likely had him in an "ESL" type of program (except for the language being learned was Japanese of course) and they worked on improving his spoken language skills, and devoted a smaller degree of time to written.

Without extended formalized schooling, his spoken ability would be limited to common daily topics and interests. Assuming that he was without a professional translator readily available to him that could help him with the language, it would be extremely hard to learn new vocabulary and sophisticated means of communication. Note that I stress sophisticated.

I can attest to this as I have learned two languages in two different manners. The first language I learned was Cantonese (a Chinese dialect) when I was 10 years old. I learned this language verbally through my foster family. I came to some command of the language, but was only understanding what was said in a family environment (conversations around food, shopping, the day at work, etc.). So if I was watching a Cantonese show, I would more or less not understand most of the complicated topics, but if it was a show about family situations, I would be okay. I never learned to read or write Chinese, which was another major hindrance to my becoming more advanced in the language.

The second language I learned was Japanese, which I learned when I attended Penn State University. I learned this language in the classical manner, with reading and writing being primary topics as well as spoken, and came to a greater degree of mastery because of it. When I was a student in Japan I could carry on conversations with individuals on a great number of topics, something I could not do in Chinese.

This certainly must have been a factor in the case for Choi Yong-Sool, and I imagine that his command of Japanese would be adequate for most common situations, but for more advanced topics (such as talking about Japanese history), it would be extremely difficult to comprehend without the benefit of translation.

The frustration levels for Choi Yong-Sool would build and build, from perhaps being ostracized or bullied at school, struggling with the language and customs of a foreign land. I am positive that he longed to return to his homeland. The frustration would be taken out on other students by fighting, which he himself attests to in his biography. The more he fought, the more he wanted to learn how to get better at it. Combine this with the temple's murals that depicted war scenes and martial arts, Choi Yong-Sool's interest and desire to enter the martial way of life is an obvious one.

Failure

Typical Japanese Elementary School

Fortunately, the temple monk Kintaro Watanabe realized Choi Yong-Sool's desire and confirmed this with him through extended conversations. The monk was an alleged friend or acquaintance of master Sokaku Takeda, the head of the Daito-Ryu Aiki-Jujutsu martial arts system located in northern Japan.

The Daito-Ryu Aiki JuJutsu is a Japanese martial arts system that emphasizes empty handed methods that are based on the many martial styles of the Samurai warriors. Many of the samurai families fled to northern Japan with their leader, the last Shogun (Tokugawa), and were permitted to settle in estates in the northern prefectures by the Emperor of the Meiji Restoration.

Dai   To   Ryu

Breaking down the name of the system, Daito-Ryu Aiki JuJutsu, I am translating into English from the Japanese characters. This is <u>my</u> translation of the characters and their meaning:

Daito-Ryu = Great Eastern Flow/School
Aiki = Synchronized Energy
JuJutsu = Soft Art

From the Daito-Ryu materials, the translation they give is "Great Eastern School of Martial Arts"

The origins of Daito-Ryu maintain a direct lineage extending approximately 900 years, from the Minamoto samurai clan. The originator of the art, Shinra Saburo Minamoto no Yoshimitsu (a member of the Minamoto family descended from the 56th emperor of Japan – Emperor Seiwa), originally founded the art and named it Daito-Ryu after the home he lived in as a child. While this is not a complete, detailed history of Daito-Ryu Aiki JuJutsu, it sums up what is needed for this book. Further reading can be found in the bibliography of this book.

Yoshimitsu's great grandson Nobuyoshi changed his surname to "Takeda", which has been carried on by the family to modern times. Therefore Sokaku Takeda's family was one of the ancient samurai families that lived in this northern area and maintained their martial arts system, and Sokaku was the master of the system at the time Choi Yong-Sool was in Japan.

It is at this point that there are conflicts in the life story of Choi Yong-Sool and how he came to learn Daito-Ryu Aiki JuJutsu.

ai   ki

Master Sokaku Takeda

LIFE WITH MASTER TAKEDA

In Choi Yong-Sool's biography and interviews, he has stated that he was adopted by the Takeda family when he was 11 years old and given the name Asao Yoshida (other sources state Tatsujutsu Yoshida). He lived with the family, calling Sokaku "Father" for 30 years and was taught the Daito-Ryu Aiki JuJutsu system, in which he became a master.

Other sources claim that he was a servant in the household, and attended seminars that were held by Sokaku Takeda, and learned the art through these seminars. The founder of Aikido, Morihei Ueshiba, who was a registered student of Takeda's, told his son (Kisshomaru) that Choi Yong-Sool attended seminars held by Takeda but was not a registered student.

*Aikido founder and Daito Ryu master
Morihei Ueshiba*

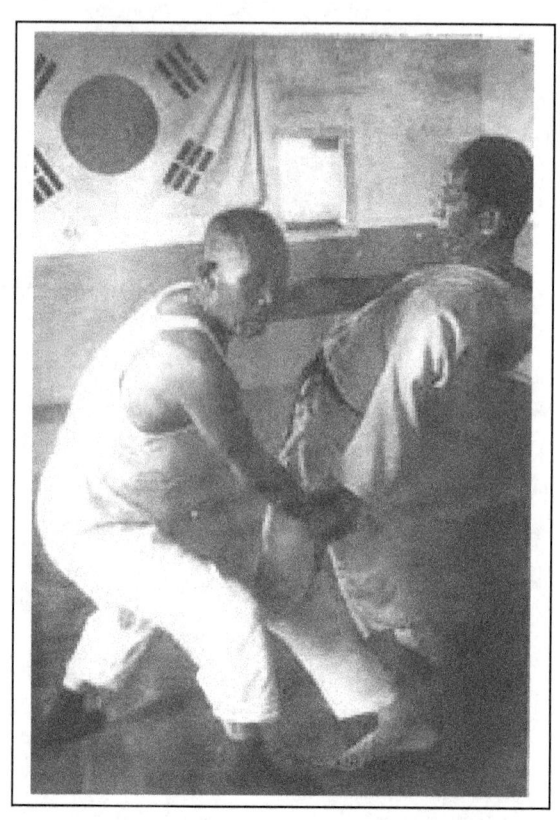

Master Choi during training session

The Takeda family kept meticulous records of who the registered students were, what techniques they were taught, and how much they paid. None of the names given by Choi Yong-Sool, neither his Korean name, nor Tatsujutsu/Asao Yoshida, are on these records. There are names of other Korean's on the registration rolls, but not Choi Yong-Sool's.

Of course this does not invalidate his claim to be living with the Takeda family and having trained with them. It could very well be that he was indeed living with the family in some form, and that he either trained off-hours with Master Takeda (so as not to be charge), perhaps watched the classes/training and then worked on the techniques with other house-mates, or learned the techniques at the seminars as stated.

Choi Yong-Sool was eventually given the Japanese name of Asao Yoshida (and some sources state the first name was "Tatsujutsu"). To me this represents a significant shift in his relationship with the Takeda family. His being given a Japanese name certainly reflects that he was in favor with the family, as they chose to narrow the gap with his Korean birth and living with a native born Japanese family. I can see where if Choi Yong-Sool worked hard, was dependable, was young, was moldable, he could indeed come into the family's favor.

Does this mean that he was an adoptive son? In the end it is all speculative. That he was given a Japanese name is very significant, and it is very possible that he called Master Takeda "Otosan".

The term "father" in Japanese is used a bit more freely than how it is used in western cultures. While I was an exchange student in Japan, I was permitted to call my host family's father "Otoosan", which literally means father. Now, due to the fact that I am from the western culture, I do not claim literally that my host father was my "father", I usually clarify it by stating he was my "host family father" or similar.

I can see though, that someone whose native language is not English or other western language, would state plainly that he was "father", or that I called him father. This statement then, in the western mind and interpretation, brings along the family concept and we then assume a very close relationship, which may or may not be the actual case.

Happiness

However being allowed to refer to Master Takeda as "Otoosan" is significant even if it does not mean that he was his actual father or adoptive father. What it tells me is that Master Choi was allowed into the circle of trust and was close with the family and Master Takeda.

Let's take a look at how he came to be with the Takeda family and the different options he had for learning the art.

For him to get to Akita from Osaka is a matter we need to look at. He certainly could not have traveled on his own, with little or no money, and if he did, it would have been such an adventure I am positive he would have talked about it. No, the most likely scenario is that he was picked up and brought to Akita by the Takeda family as he was to work for them.

At this point, we have a good understanding of his early stay in Japan, and now we will investigate some scenarios as to how Choi Yong-Sool most likely came to live with the Takeda family. We know that he was in Japan, that has been proven. We know that he was directed towards Master Takeda to learn the martial art of Daito-Ryu Aiki JuJutsu by his temple monk master. But how did he get all the way to the Takeda's family's residence?

At the time it is assumed he had little or no money, remember just a few years prior he was on the streets begging, he had little or no education, and no trade skills. If he were to make his way to Akita, the site of the Takeda residence which is in northern Japan, he would need to travel a distance of 550 miles. From Osaka, he would need to travel west to Kyoto and then along the western coast of Japan heading north until he came to Akita. This is no easy task.

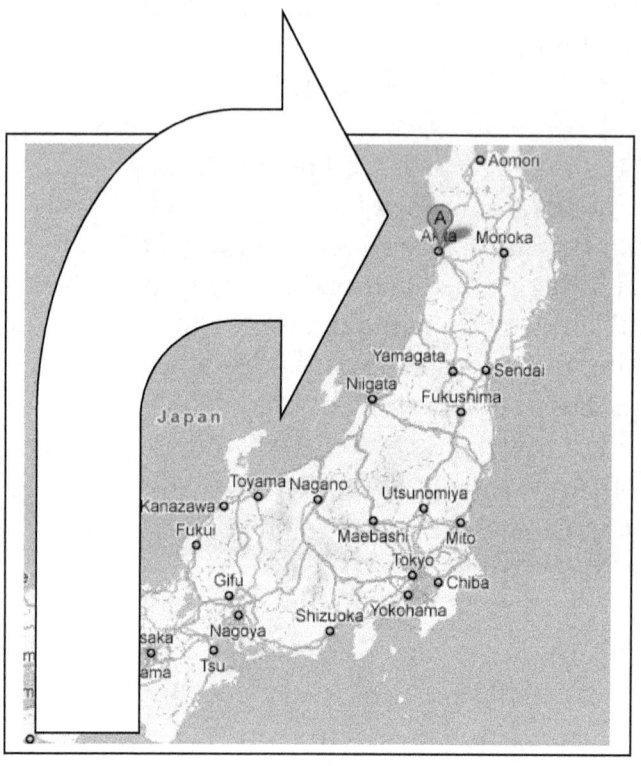

So the question is how did he get there. I am fairly certain that he did not hitch hike his way there, and it was also unlikely for a Japanese person to take a troubled Korean-born youth 550 miles north for free. It is possible that Choi Yong-Sool made the journey by himself on foot, subsiding on handouts as he made the journey. But we certainly would have heard something about this from him in his biography if it happened in this manner.

My feeling is that he was taken there as a laborer for the Takeda family initially.

First, lets figure out the time line. Choi Yong-Sool was in Japan at the age of 8. At 11 years old he claims to be living with the Takeda family, which would put us at 1915. The timeline then looks like this.

Time Line: Choi Yong-Sool
1904: born in Korea
1912: taken to Japan (8 years old)
1912 – 1914: time spent in temple (2 years as per his biography), now 10 years old
1914-1915: travel to Akita
1915: in residence with Takeda family (11 years old)

So our time line works out for Choi Yong-Sool. Now lets take a look at the time line for Master Sokaku Takeda, to see if they align.

Time Line: Sokaku Takeda
1859: born in Japan
1875: travel to Satsuma Japan to fight in the rebellion (Meiji), age 16 years old
1875 – 1885: lived in Osaka with master swordsman Momonoi Shunzo.
1885: return to Akita

So in 1914 it is relatively safe to assume that Master Takeda, then age 55 years old, would be living in Akita.

That Master Takeda lived in Osaka for ten years adds credence to the claim by monk Watanabe to have known him and it is entirely possible for a friendship to have developed, as was claimed.

We can then extrapolate that monk Watanabe was in contact with the Takeda family, and offered the services of Choi Yong-Sool. Upon acceptance, the Takeda family would arrange for transportation for the young man to be taken to Akita.

It is certainly likely that Choi Yong-Sool was initially a day laborer or handy man, worker of some sort for the Takeda family initially. This should not be taken as a discouraging remark. When we look at the situation in its entirety, where was young, he had no money, no professional skills, and was not Japanese, then we are left with what he could offer, and that was manual labor.

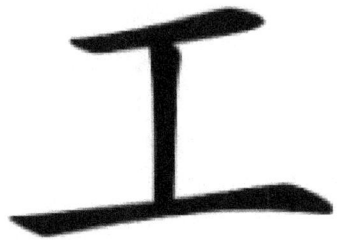

Work

VALIDITY OF CLAIMS AND RECORDS

The significance of his being there is in the final determination of how, when and where he received his training. I am almost certain that master Choi was not an "official" paying student of master Takeda. What this means simply is that master Choi was not paying for the lessons as the other students were, such as Master Ueshiba. This, combined with the statement of Master Ueshiba that Master Choi was not a registered student, for me confirms this matter.

What is confirmed though is that Master Choi did indeed learn the techniques of Daito-Ryu Aiki JuJutsu, now the question is how and what exactly did he learn.

My first inclination is that he learned privately. Under this scenario initially Master Choi was permitted to watched the classes and learned though observation, which was the most common method of martial arts training in the past for young apprentices, where they would not enter the dojo for at least two years and were kept on the outside looking in, and then their job was to clean, fix and perform other menial tasks after the training was complete. If they were obedient and dependable, they would be invited in to train after the allotted period of time passed.

Master Choi would certainly be in this group. While not an official apprentice, he most likely observed and worked with the other apprentices after the training had finished. I can envision Master Takeda, knowing full well that Master Choi would not be able to afford his lessons, but seeing the desire that the young man had, may teach Master Choi privately.

In addition, it is possible that he would travel with the family to the seminars. Especially if Master Choi were a close personal employee of the family. He would be brought along to assist the family and Master Takeda, and certainly would be allowed to participate in the seminars. Especially if he was being privately trained and could act as a training partner/demonstration assistant ("Uki") for Master Takeda. Then you can see the benefit Master Takeda would realize with Master Choi, here is a person that will be coming along with him at all times, and he would be the perfect disciple to train as an Uki for the seminars. It is also possible that he was allowed to take the seminars for free due to his relationship with the family. It is also possible that he saved his earnings and used it to pay for the seminars (which is highly likely).

Now Master Takeda had his students that traveled with him, and would assist him at the seminar, that is true. But having Choi with him meant that he did not need to rely on one of his students always being with him as he traveled about. With Choi at his side at all times, he would have a fit and able Uki apprentice to demonstrate techniques. It has been confirmed from an outside source that Master Choi was with Master Takeda at the seminars as Aikido's Master Ueshiba himself stated that Master Choi was indeed present at the seminars.

To further cement the proof that Master Choi learned the techniques of Daito-Ryu Aiki JuJutsu, lets look at three techniques that are the basis of Daito-Ryu Aiki JuJutsu wrist locks, as well as Hapkido and Aikido.

THREE BASIC DAITO-RYU AIKI JUJUTSU TECHNIQUES LEARNED

There are three techniques that we are going to look at. They were chosen because of their uniqueness (gripping style) to Daito-Ryu Aiki JuJutsu, but also because they are found in the systems of Aikido as well as Hapkido.

Daito-Ryu Aiki JuJutsu, like other forms of jujutsu, emphasizes throwing techniques and joint manipulations to effectively control, subdue, or injure an attacker.

These three locks are also the fundamental basis for nearly all the throws and submission techniques found in the other two systems. In Daito-Ryu Aiki JuJutsu, techniques are broken up in to specific lists, which are then trained sequentially, meaning that a student will not progress to the next set of techniques until he has mastered the previous one.

This is today true in Hapkido and Aikido. Upon completion of each level, a student is given a scroll that lists the techniques at that level, and was used as a means of advancement, much as belts are used today. Therefore we can look to see that techniques are going to be listed, or numbered, and will proceed in progression.

	Catalogue Name	No. of Techniques
1	Secret Syllabus (秘伝目録 Hiden Mokuroku?)	118
2	The Science of Joining Spirit (合気之術 Aiki-no-jutsu?)	53
3	Inner Mysteries (秘伝奥義 Hiden Ōgi?)[124]	36
4	Techniques of Self Defense (護身用の手 Goshin'yō-no-te?)[125]	84
5	Explanation of the Inheritance (解釈相伝 Kaishaku Sōden?)	477
6	License of Complete Transmission (Menkyo Kaiden)	88

What makes these three wrist lock techniques unique, as compared to the same locks found in other systems and styles (including western wrestling) is the use of the hand when gripping. All three systems use the base of the hand starting at the little finger and working its way up to grip the wrist (in any of the three locks), with the pointer finger usually not being the primary holder involved directly with the grip or even extended outwards pointing away. This style of gripping is based on the way a katana (sword) is held by the Japanese Samurai, and carried over to the Daito-Ryu Aiki JuJutsu system.

PRONATING WRIST LOCK

The first basic lock is the Pronating Wrist lock, or the forearm turn (Kote Mawashi) in Japanese. This is the "Nikyo" of Aikido, and can be basically equivalent to "Oht 3 Soo" of Dr. He-Young Kimm's Hapkido manual in terms of the grip. The pronating wrist lock is termed "Nikyo" in Aikido, which translated loosely means second teaching. This is important as Aikido reflects Daito-Ryu Aiki JuJutsu in many aspects, and the basic fundamental locks can be assumed to be closely tied to Master Takeda's teaching and the order they were taught in. This is reflected in Hapkido's "Oht 3 Soo" or 3rd defense against a cloth seize, again being one of the fundamental movements. The grip is also found in the Son Mok Soo - defense against wrist seize, another basic technique taught.

The pronating wrist lock is where the hand is maximally pronated, which creates a joint lock on the wrist and the radio ulnar joint. The opponent's hand is gripped by either the left or right hand, and turned so that the opponent's base (pinky finger base) is pointing skywards. The grip itself is important, with the thumb on the inside of the opponent's palm, with the pinky, ring and middle finger's applying the pressure to maintain the grip. The wrist is then pronated to the maximum extent. This lock then can be added to additional techniques and locks, such as extending or bending the elbow, or turning the shoulder, or applying pressure to the bicep - the list goes on but all work back to the basic lock.

Pronating Wrist Lock Examples (Aiki-JuJutsu, Hapkido)

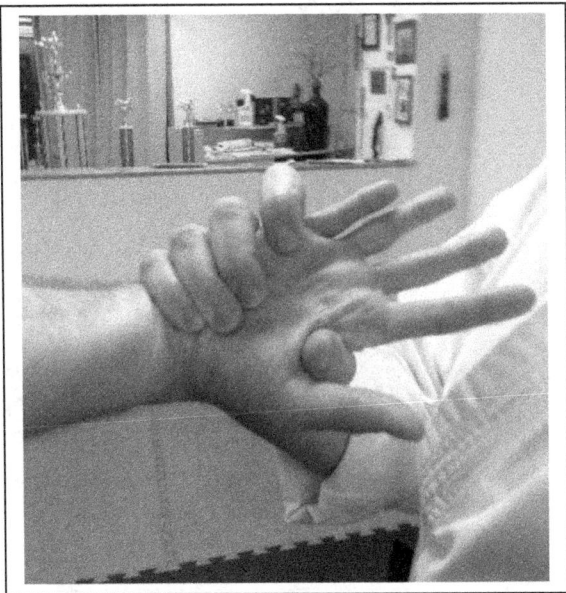

Initial Aiki-JuJutsu grip. Note the location of the index finger. The bottom three fingers maintain the steadfast hold.

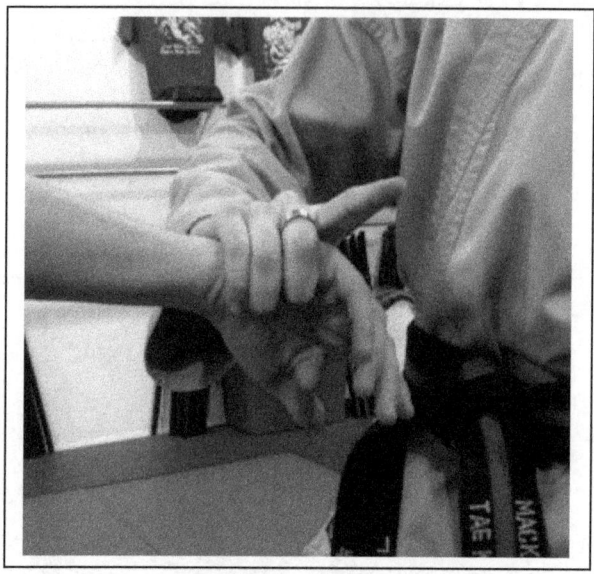

Initial Hapkido (Sin Moo Hapkido)
grip, note the extended index finger.

SUPINATING WRIST LOCK

The second lock we will look at is the Supinating Wrist Lock, or the forearm return (Kote Gaeshi) in Japanese. This technique can be found in all three systems (Aikido uses the same Japanese term, and Dr. Kimm lists this technique as Oht 8 Soo).

The supinating wrist lock is a rotational wrist lock, where the hand is turned until is is maximally supinated, with the thumb pointing away from the opponent. The opponent's hand is gripped with either the left or right hand, with the thumb on the back of the hand, and the three base gripping fingers grabbing the fat portion beneath the opponent's thumb (unless the gripping hand is the same side, which would mean that the gripping base would be along the pinky ridge). As the wrist is turned to the maximum supination, the opponent will either turn/fall/roll to relieve the pressure, or the wrist, shoulder will be broken or the elbow dislocated.

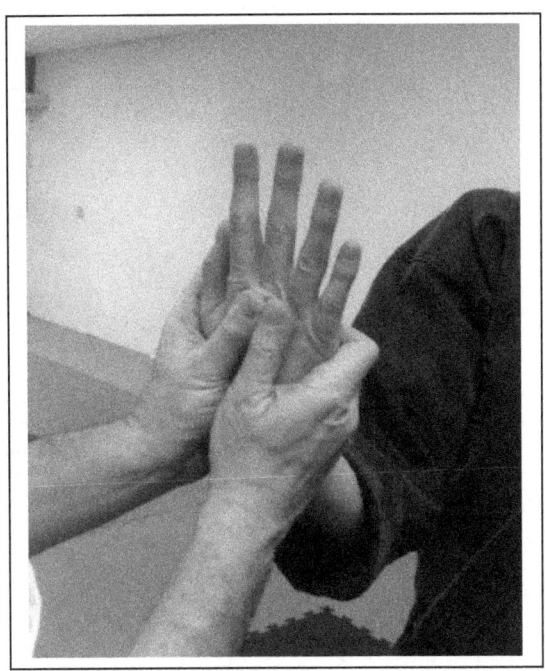

The Aiki-JuJutsu grip for the supinating wrist lock is the "sandwich" grip, with thumbs together on the back side of the hand.

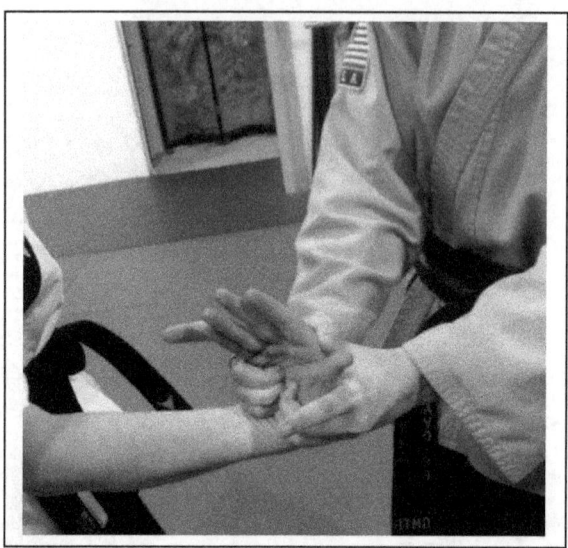

Notice the index fingers being extended. Also note the location of the thumb.

ROTATIONAL WRIST LOCK

The third common (base) technique we will look at is the rotational wrist lock, noted as "Ikkyo" and "Sankyo" in Aikido (first and third teachings), and can be found in many other of the Daito-Ryu Aiki JuJutsu, Aikido and Hapkido curriculums listed in many different ways (Oht 9 Soo and "Z-Lock" for example).

The rotational wrist lock is the forced pronation or supination of the wrist, with a joint lock on the radio ulnar joint, and placing the radius and ulna in their extreme positions, which puts severe torque on the wrist. While it is indeed the same movements and techniques as the pronating and supinating locks, the real difference here is the addition of an extra joint manipulation that creates the leverage, as seen in these examples.

All three of these wrist locks are found in all three systems (Daito-Ryu Aiki JuJutsu, Aikido and Hapkido), and due to their similarity in naming conventions, gripping styles, and additional extensions, we can therefore assume that they were learned from the same original source (Master Takeda).

This strong similarity to the techniques taught in Daito-Ryu Aiki JuJutsu, Aikido and the Hapkido add strenght to the claim that Master Choi did indeed learn the base JuJutsu techniques from Master Takeda as he claims.

RETURN TO KOREA AND INITIAL DEVELOPMENT

At some point in 1945 Master Choi returned to Korea. He is said to have taken a ship to Pusan, and then a train to Tae Ku City, which is where he lost the bag containing his money, clothes and his Daito-Ryu Aiki JuJutsu certificates, and the controversy is born.

In order to be a master of Daito-Ryu Aiki JuJutsu, one needs to be awarded the Menkyo Kaiden, as shown in the diagram below.

	Catalogue Name	No. of Techniques
1	Secret Syllabus (秘伝目録 Hiden Mokuroku?)	118
2	The Science of Joining Spirit (合気之術 Aiki-no-jutsu?)	53
3	Inner Mysteries (秘伝奥義 Hiden Ōgi?)[124]	36
4	Techniques of Self Defense (護身用の手 Goshin'yō-no-te?)[126]	84
5	Explanation of the Inheritance (解釈相伝 Kaishaku Sōden?)	477
6	License of Complete Transmission (Menkyo Kaiden)	88

There have been only three Menkyo Kaiden awarded in Daito-Ryu's history, and Master Choi was not listed on Daito-Ryu's records as being one of the recipients. There were many more teaching licenses (kyoju dairi) issued by Daito-Ryu, but it can not be confirmed as to whether or not Master Choi received one of these because the lists of recipients held by the Daito-Ryu Kodokai (or the Roppokai) are not available for public viewing, and both organizations do not allow for examination of their records by outside parties.

Important note is that Master Morihei Ueshiba, the founder of Aikido and long time student of Master Takeda, was the recipient of the Hiden Mokuroko, Hiden Ogi, Goshin yo-no-te as well as the kyoju dairi (teaching) certificates.

Unless these record holding facilities are opened and examined by independent scholars, the matter as to what exactly Master Choi had taken from him at that train station, and the exact level of Daito-Ryu mastery he obtained, will remain a mystery.

With no money, Master Choi was stuck in Tai Ku where he first worked as a bread salesman, and after a year (1946) he had saved enough money to start a pig farm. He would go daily to the Suh Brewery Company to obtain the free grain they would dispense. It was on one of these days that he was in a scuffle in the waiting yard, and the son of the chairman of the brewery, Suh Bok-Sup, saw him and brought him in to train.

The intent of this book is not to review the history of Hapkido from the point of the meeting between these two, there is amble documentation in this regard. What this book's intent is to focus on the validity of the training master Choi received, and we can further investigate this by looking at the system he taught early.

Lets look first at what Master Choi initially called his system. When Master Suh initially created space in the brewery for training, the system name that they were training was called, in Korean, "Dai Dong Ryu Yu Kwon Sool", very similar to Daito-Ryu Aiki JuJutsu but using Korean words. It is important to note here that the word "Aiki" (or Hapki in Korean) was left out (I will discuss this later on). The name was then shortened to "Yu Sool" by Master Choi, whereas Master Suh kept it "Yu Kwon Sool" when he began teaching his own students at a later time. Master Choi might have shortened the name to make it easier for his students to remember, or perhaps the "Dai Dong Ryu" was too "Japanese" for the Korean's tastes, but this is all speculative.

Yu Sool loosely translates to JuJutsu in Japanese, meaning "Soft Art". Yu Kwon Sool would mean "Soft Art Striking with the Hand."

Aiki as a Japanese word is translated "HapKi" in Korean, with both meanings being the same (they use the same Chinese characters), meaning "Meeting/Being in Sync, harmonious spirit" for "Ai" and "Energy" for "Ki", so "synchronized energy" is a good English translation. To pull when you are pushed, to push when you are pulled, these are some basic interpretations of Aiki.

I will discuss more about "Aiki" in the next section of this book.

Now if our assumption that Master Choi studied Daito-Ryu Aiki JuJutsu, then there is absolutely no doubt that he knew the Korean way of pronouncing/transcribing the Japanese would be "Dai Dong Ryu HapKi Yu Sool". Even if he was illiterate, he would still know how to pronounced in Korean his founders school system and name.

However, that he shortened it to Yu Sool (JuJutsu) shows that he might have been not so concerned as to what his "style" was called, rather, he wanted a generic name that all would be able to quickly understand. But this could also be interpreted as meaning that he understood that he did not learn the entire Daito-Ryu curriculum, and therefore shortened his school style name to what he did learn, JuJutsu.

The teaching of Daito-Ryu can be broken into three levels. The first is the teaching of JuJutsu, this is then moved to Aiki-no-JuJutsu, and then followed by Aiki JuJutsu. The first, JuJutsu is the "hard/soft" techniques and can be classified as the joint locking techniques. The next level, Aiki-no-JuJutsu translates as "the hard/soft techniques of synchronized energy" or as written in the official Daito-Ryu catalog as "Science of Joining Spirit". Finally, the third level, Aiki JuJutsu translates as "synchronized hard/soft techniques".

These groupings, and their techniques incorporated into them, take many years to master. It takes, on average, 10-15 years to learn all three groups. Master Choi was most certainly in Japan for the required amount of time to learn all these.

One item that is perplexing and spoken of in great detail by the Daito-Ryu and Aikido schools about their relationship with Hapkido, but will not be covered in this book, is the lack of Japanese sword techniques that are taught in Daito-Ryu but not found in Hapkido. My comment on this is that swords and the possession of them was illegal in Korea after the war, and therefore Master Choi would not have taught techniques, if he knew them, for something that was illegal.

What possible gain would he have to teach sword techniques that were illegal in his home country. There is none. So he would have simply abandoned them and not have included them in his curriculum.

Unfortunately, this is a question that will need to remain unresolved as we have no way of knowing what Master Choi was taught in regards to the sword.

Master Ueshiba, the founder of Aikido, received his Kashima Shinden Jikishinkage-Ryu sword transmission scroll from Master Takeda in 1922, and the sword techniques were later incorporated into Aikido. Master Ueshiba though, lived in Japan, with different laws.

Master Ji, Han Jae

JI HAN JAE'S CONTRIBUTIONS AND DEVELOPMENT

Grandmaster Ji Han Jae began studing with Master Choiat Master Choi's private residence, and became student #14of Master Choi sometime between the years 1953 and 1955.
It was Grandmaster Ji Han Jae who decided to use the word "do" – meaning "way", and changed Hapki Yu Kwon Sool to what we call today "Hapkido". This was confirmed by the Korean government when they listed Grandmaster Ji Han Jae as the founder of "Hapkido".

Grandmaster Ji Han Jae then added in the various other techniques he learned from other systems (such as kicking, striking and weapons) and brought the art to Seoul, where the art exploded in popularity.

All systems and branches of Daito-Ryu Aiki JuJutsu need to recognize and give credit to where it is due to master Ji Han Jae. His popularization of the art of Hapkido has directly led to the success and popularity of Aikido and Aiki JuJutsu. Without his selfless and tireless efforts, all three arts would not enjoy the recognition that they have today.

I can not stress enough the importance that master Ji Han Jae's popularization of the arts had in the world wide community. His role in the Bruce Lee movie, "Game of Death", attracted significant recognition and inquiry into the art and their roots, which led to Aikido and Aiki-JuJutsu receiving similar interest.

Why did master Ji Han Jae create the name "Hapkido" and shorten it?

One of the reasons for the name change (from Yu Kwon Sul – JuJutsu) was the addition of striking and kicking techniques that Grandmaster Ji Han Jae added to the system. Much of the curriculum and techniques that are associated with Hapkido today are heavily marked by the changes that were implemented by Grandmaster Ji Han Jae.

Several years later, Grandmaster Ji Han Jae began to look at the spiritual side of Hapkido, and incorporated mediation into the art. Emphasis given to the meditative, philosophical and Ki development training. Interesting to note that Master Ueshiba also went through a similar transition.

He also began exploring the "Aiki" of Hapkido. As with Aikido and Aiki-JuJutsu, the Aiki portion plays a significant role.

This becomes important in the next section, the use of Aiki in Hapkido.

Hapkido

MODERN DAY HAPKIDO AND THE USE OF AIKI

Nothing seems to get people all worked up from the opposing groups (Daito-Ryu Aiki JuJutsu, Aikido, Hapkido) then the discussion of the use of "Aiki" (harmonious spirit) in these arts.

If you had 15 different instructors from each of these styles, you would probably come away with 45 different interpretations and arguments.

There is no getting around the fact that there are numerous so-called "instructors" out there with dubious credentials. But by staying with the founders, as I have done with this book, we can circumvent any misleading problems.

I am not going to attempt to say one style is right, the other is wrong. Nor am I going to argue who has "Aiki" and who doesn't. I am also not going to argue whose "Aiki" is used the way the founder intended and whose does not.

This book is simply going to show that "Aiki" is integrated in modern day Hapkido.

Lets take a look first at "JuJutsu" as a whole. The basic emphasis is an early neutralization of an attack, emphasizing throwing techniques and joint manipulations to effectively control, subdue, or use the force of the attacker's movement against them. Daito-ryu is characterized by ample use of atemi, or the striking of vital areas, in order to set up joint locking or throwing tactics. Aikido and Hapkido share all of this.

Master Takeda defined "Aiki" as "to over power the opponent mentally at a glance and to win without fighting".

Master Takeda's son, Tokimune, further elaborated on "Aiki": "*Aiki is to pull when you are pushed, and to push when you are pulled. It is the spirit of slowness and speed, of harmonizing your movement with your opponent's ki. Its opposite, kiai, is to push to the limit, while aiki never resists. The term aiki has been used since ancient times and is not unique to Daito-ryu. The ki in aiki is 'go no sen', meaning to respond to an attack.*"

He continues:

"... Daito-ryu is all 'go no sen' – you first evade your opponent's attack and then strike or control him. You attack because an opponent attacks you. This implies not cutting your opponent. This is called katsujinken (life-giving sword). Its opposite is called setsuninken (death-dealing sword)."

And concludes:
"...Aiki is different from the victory, and is applied in situations of 'go no sen', such as when an opponent thrusts at you. Therein lies the essence of katsujinken and setsuninken. You block the attack when an opponent approaches; at his second attack you break his sword and spare his life. This is katsujinken. When an opponent strikes at you and your sword pierces his stomach it is setsuninken. These two concepts are the essence of the sword."

Aikido also interprets "Aiki" in a similar way. Master Ueshiba had an "enlightening" in 1925, as follows by this excert: "Master Ueshiba had defeated a naval officer's bokken (wooden katana) attacks unarmed and without hurting the officer. Ueshiba then walked to his garden and had a spiritual awakening.

'At that moment I was enlightened: the source of budo (martial way) is God's love - the spirit of loving protection for all beings... Budo is not the felling of an opponent by force; nor is it a tool to lead the world to destruction with arms. True Budo is to accept the spirit of the universe, keep the peace of the world, correctly produce, protect and cultivate all beings in nature'"

Thus, the "Aiki" found in both Daito-Ryu and Aikido have very similar meanings and goals.

Is this found in Hapkido? I believe the answer is yes.

Grandmaster Ji Han Jae explains the meaning of Hapkido. "Hap" means bringing together, gathering or harmonizing. "Ki" is the energy or breath in the body that connects the mind and the body. "Do" is the process or way this happens. The definition of Hapkido then, according to Grandmaster Ji Han Jae, is *"the way of harmonizing the mind and body through the utilization of ki"*.

In 1983 in Seoul, South Korea, Grandmaster Ji Han Jae founded "Sin Moo Hapkido", with "Sin" meaning "higher mind/spirit" and "Moo" translating as "martial art". The new system then can be translated as "The way of using martial arts to harmonize the mind and body to reach a higher more enlightened state of existence".

Grandmaster Ji Han Jae's Sin Moo Hapkido organization: "The way of using martial arts to harmonize the mind and body to reach a higher more enlightened state of existence" – this certainly reflects "Aiki" teachings to me.

It also closely aligns itself, and even surpasses Master Takeda's original message – to win without fighting.

In conclusion, I must determine that Aiki is indeed included in Hapkido.

The End

CONCLUSION

This book analyzed Hapkido master Choi Yong-Sool's claim to have studied directly under Daito-Ryu Aiki JuJutsu master Sokaku Takeda, and why this claim to have studied directly from the Takeda family's Daito-Ryu Aiki JuJutsu system is important to establishing not only his legitimacy in teaching the martial art, but also to trace the common roots that Daito-Ryu Aiki JuJutsu, Hapkido and Aikido share by tracing his lineage back to the root tradition.

This book looked at master Choi Yong-Sool's early history, as compiled from his own biography as well as external sources, it compared and contrasted three critical and fundamental techniques used in Hapkido, Aikido and Aiki-JuJutsu and traced them back to Daito-Ryu Aiki-Jutsu.

It is well known that master Choi Yong-Sool's biography, interview and assertions of having studied Daito-Ryu Aiki JuJutsu has caused great controversy in Daito-Ryu and other Aiki JuJutsu circles.

Are there concrete facts, a paper trail that we can follow to dispel this controversy? No. But there are many arguments and proofs that can be attained that show what is said to have happened indeed happened. In fact, for most academic historical purposes, there is enough information available to assert these claims as facts.

I believe that this book shows that Hapkido practitioners and instructors can feel confident in their history and legacy. For those looking to find the origins of their art and get hit in the face with the controversies that are out there, they can use the arguments in this book to present a strong case as to their roots.

This book set out to help the trace the valid history of Hapkido and help mend bridges so that organizations and instructors of Hapkido will understand their roots and in addition will help increase relationships between the various related practices that have stemmed from the parent art (Daito-Ryu Aiki JuJutsu), such as Aiki-JuJutsu and Aikido.

It is my sincere hope that this is the end result of my book.

BIBLIOGRAPHY

Kimm, He-Young (1991). Hapkido. Baton Rouge, LA: Andrew Jackson College Press.

Kaiser, Stephen (1991). Introduction to the Japanese Writing System. In Kodansha's Compact Kanji Guide. Tokyo: Kondansha International. ISBN 4-7700-1553-4.

Pranin, Stanley (2006). "Daito-Ryu Aikijujutsu". Encyclopedia of Aikido. Retrieved 2007-07-20

Pranin, Stanley (1996). Daito-ryu Aikijujutsu: Conversations with Daito-ryu Masters. Tokyo: Aiki News. ISBN 4900586188.

Draeger, Donn F. (February 1, 1996). Modern Bujutsu & Budo: The Martial Arts and Ways of Japan, Volume Three. Boston, Massachusetts: Weatherhill. ISBN 978-0834803510.

Websites:

http://www.aikidojournal.com/ubb/Forum32/HTML/000003.html

http://www.beckmartialarts.com/chkdfaq.html
http://www.americanhapkidoacademy.com/2007SITEUPDATE/hapkido.htm
http://en.wikipedia.org - Choi Yong-Sool
http://en.wikipedia.org - Daito-Ryu Aiki JuJutsu

Photographs:

Aiki JuJutsu Pronating, Supinating, Rotational Lock Examples:
Mark Dzikiy
Grant M. Miller, 5th degree, Shotokan, Aiki Jutsu, Aikido and Hapkido

Hapkido Pronating, Supinating, Rotational Lock Examples:
W. Vaughn LaVoice, 4th degree, Sin Moo Hapkido
Michael Justice, Shodan, Sin Moo Hapkido

CPSIA information can be obtained
at www.ICGtesting.com
Printed in the USA
LVHW081312030919
629778LV00013B/563/P